Let's Talk About Pagan Elements and the Wheel of the Year

Let's Talk About Pagan Elements and the Wheel of the Year

Siusaidh Ceanadach

Winchester, UK
Washington, USA

First published by Moon Books, 2013
Moon Books is an imprint of John Hunt Publishing Ltd., Laurel House, Station Approach,
Alresford, Hants, SO24 9JH, UK
office1@jhpbooks.net
www.johnhuntpublishing.com
www.moon-books.net

For distributor details and how to order please visit the 'Ordering' section on our website.

Text and illustrations copyright: Siusaidh Ceanadach 2012

ISBN: 978 1 78099 561 8

All rights reserved. Except for brief quotations in critical articles or reviews, no part of this
book may be reproduced in any manner without prior written permission from the publishers.

The rights of Siusaidh Ceanadach as author have been asserted in accordance with the
Copyright, Designs and Patents Act 1988.

A CIP catalogue record for this book is available from the British Library.

Design: Stuart Davies

Printed and bound by CPI Group (UK) Ltd, Croydon, CR0 4YY

We operate a distinctive and ethical publishing philosophy in all
areas of our business, from our global network of authors to
production and worldwide distribution.

CONTENTS

Questions and Answers

Introduction to the Elements

In the first 'Let's Talk' book we covered the eight festivals of the Wheel of the Year, the solar festivals and the fire festivals or cross quarter festivals. Let's take this one step further now and bring in the four elements which are linked to directions, bringing them into their place on the Pagan Wheel of the Year. If you haven't read the first 'Let's Talk' book there is no need to worry, you don't have to read both books. I will explain a bit about the festivals of the Wheel of the Year later in this book too.

First let me introduce the classical elements.

There are four classical elements; Air, Fire, Water and Earth and the fifth element is the unseen one, Spirit. Spirit comes into everything and is symbolised by the circle; the unseen super-natural protection that we feel comes from the flow of the Universal Spirit, or Awen or Holy Spirit. In Judeo/Christian terms the word translates to 'spirit' or 'wisdom' so it would seem that humans came to the same understanding in the Middle East as we did here in Europe.

The classical elements we use today come from the ancient Greek civilization and were used in Europe in the Middle Ages in the development of alchemy, which was the beginnings of early science.

Let's look into the classical elements, starting with 'Air'.

Air is linked to the direction of East here in Britain, but the direction can change depending on where you live. The colour yellow is the main colour for the Air and the East and this symbolises light, wind/breeze, freshness and mental agility. Subjects linked to Air include mathematics and music. This element is also linked on the Wheel of the Year to the spring, from the first very early awakening of spring moving, as the year turns on, to the Spring Equinox or Vernal Equinox, also known as Ostara.

The kind of colour yellow linked to the element of Air is a sharp citrus yellow, the colour of daffodils. The season bursts into colour around the third week of March here in Britain, but if you live in the southern hemisphere then it's going to be about the third week of September.

Everywhere in the town gardens, in the city parks and by the sides of the roads in the countryside bright yellow flowers come into bloom, followed about a week or so later by their white, orange-centred cousins. You can measure the year in flowers; very early spring brings us the pure white snowdrops, then as the season progresses, out come the white, purple and yellow crocuses. Then the yellow daffodils, the peacock-eyed narcissi, and just a few weeks later a blue carpet of wild bluebells grace the woods, brought on by the light coming directly through the bare leafed trees to the floor of the woodland.

Everything in nature is earnest, bright, promising and eager to burst into bloom. And that is very much the feeling of this element; it's like a fresh breeze on a cold and sunny morning.

Fire is next and in Britain or Europe is linked to the South. The colour of the element Fire is red and brings passion, heat, and energy. It's the kind of passion that stops you thinking about anything else at all, takes over and gives you an overwhelming amount of energy. It is the energy that brings out the competitive spirit in us all; that drives us to win. You probably know at least one person who is very keen on playing football. There are times when all they want to do is play; they forget everything else in the passion and energy of the game. Sometimes they are so driven to win that their personality becomes more aggressive and unfriendly than they are otherwise. That is the passion of Fire taken a little too far. Controlled though, the energy of Fire helps us to keep trying to succeed in all we do.

Fire links into the summer festivals, firstly Beltane. The festival is all about the love that causes the Goddess and the God to come together. Then, in the middle of the summer, with the heat of the Sun burning down from a cloudless sky from the early hours of the morning all the way through to almost midnight, we get the Summer Solstice when our day is so long and the night never really gets dark completely. Depending on where you live, you may only get about an hour of darkness and either side a long dusk and a long dawn.

Water is usually linked to the West in Britain. The colour for Water in the classical elements is blue; any shade of blue which can be linked to the sea, the rivers, the lakes or a melting glacier. Water is very much a feeling element; it moves the soul and kindles feelings of empathy and sympathy. That is the feeling when you see your best friend in tears and you just want to hug them. You fight back the tears yourself and you can feel their sadness in your heart. Or when one of your pals has lost a member of his or her family, someone they loved, and you have such sympathy for them. They have to be so very brave and your heart goes out to them.

This is the moving power of the element of Water!

This sadness can start at Lughnasadh, the first of the autumn festivals, when the Corn King is cut down because he has to give his life in order for his people to eat throughout the coming months. We see the beautiful grain ripened under the summer Sun with the gentle breeze making a movement that looks like waves of water, it's so beautiful but it has to be cut. All you have left in the ground is a field of stubble, but you do have the grain to make bread and you have bales of straw to help feed your animals through the winter, and to spread on the ground in the barns so the cattle can sleep in comfort.

It then extends to affect the Autumn Equinox. The year has gone three parts of the way around the circle and there is sadness in the knowledge that within a few months winter will come, the leaves will drop from the trees and autumn will be upon us. Although there is a balance of light and dark at this time, it is tinged with emotion at the loss of Mother Nature's wonderful summer colours.

Earth, the element of stability, is linked to the North in Europe. It is the solid ground under our feet, the colour used for Earth is green, most of the time, although you will see either dark brown or black used as well. It just depends on where in the world you live and the colour of the ground, the soil, by you. Here in Britain, Ireland and in most of Europe you will find green is used most often, the bright green of grass.

To understand the element of Earth first we have to simply stand up, you may be in the middle of a room, but the building has its foundations in the ground and this gives it stability. Even for those who live in houses built over water, the main poles that hold the building up go down into the earth, into the ground.

Caves in the side of hills for me are one of the things I connect with the element of Earth, dark deep places, with solid floors made from the rock. The animals that make their homes in places like this are also linked to the element.

The first festival that this element touches is Samhain, with its link to the past, to our ancestors who gave us stability by passing down their genes to us. The dark colours are used at this time of the year and it is at this time of year that we often share stories, such as the tales of the mighty Cailleach who walked the hills and valleys marking them out with her huge footprints, throwing boulders around to make hills. This myth is one of the making of the land in Britain, the foundations, the very ground we walk on. It is not thought of as a factual account; it is a story that helps us feel better connected to the world we live in.

The next festival that Earth touches is the Midwinter or Yule. At Midwinter the ground is cold, often frozen, maybe even white. But although it is cold, frozen and slippery, it is still the strong foundation that helps us walk, run and jump. What would be the fun of jumping if the ground was not there to land on? As a Pagan I wait with others at Midwinter for the new-born baby God, the Sun that will eventually bring warmth and heat to the ground. Watching day by day for the increase in length of daytime light until by four days we gain between two to four minutes each day and, by the 25th, we have ten more minutes of daylight and we can see the days are getting longer. This brings stability to my day; I know how long the daylight is going to last and this means I can plan what to do.

Spirit is not part of the basic four elements because it flows in and around all of them. It is the fifth point on a pentagram and the circle around the group of people celebrating each festival. This Spirit is all through the universe. Astronauts have reported that it is not completely silent in space. There is a 'noise' a sound, and this is the sound of energy, of Spirit, the flow of what some call 'Awen', some call 'Holy Spirit'. It is a kind of supernatural energy most of the time unseen. This Spirit, this energy, can be used to guard and protect, to put life into something, to help with healing and it is almost impossible to clearly explain. You have to just accept the word of a grandmother here, Spirit is there and you can tap into it.

Strangely the Jewish/Christian Bible has a line in some editions that states: 'In the beginning was the word'. According to professors the 'word' translates as 'sound', 'noise', and it could be that what early writers were trying to say was that this sound, this energy, was within the universe right from the start. This is 'Spirit' and it is around us, was around our ancestors and will always be there, a magical flow of energy and a blanket of safety.

The Wheel of the Year

For those who do not have a background in the Pagan faith, I will go over the Wheel of the Year briefly.

The year is broken up into eight different festivals; we have touched on some of them while learning about the elements. There are four solar festivals and four fire festivals that make up the whole Wheel of the Year. In Wiccan terms these are **Sabbats**, and although the word was originally of ancient Hebrew origin, the festivals of the Wheel of the Year themselves have origins both in Celtic and in Germanic pre-Christian feasts. Two cultures have combined and melded into what is now a worldwide acceptance of the basic structure for many modern Pagans. The New Year begins and ends at Samhain, the Celtic New Year, which is one of four cross quarter festivals or fire festivals. It is a continuous flow starting and ending at Samhain, better known from a commercial view as 'Halloween'.

Samhain

In the northern hemisphere this is kept on October 31st and in the southern hemisphere it is May 1st. It's a time to celebrate the lives of those who have left this physical plane and gone on to the next. Many of us call this place the 'Summerlands'. We pay respect to our ancestors and this involves those we can trace back in our own family, our blood ancestors. It also includes those that we can trace who married or were adopted into the family and so are connected via a contract, or we say of a 'line'. And, lastly, we also celebrate those ancestors of the place where we live or work or play. We call these our ancestors 'of place'.

Pagans also often include past pets. These are also loved ones and we would remember them also at this time.

When we meet up as a group to celebrate this festival you may hear one of the members call to 'our ancestors of blood, line and place'. In my own group we make a point of reading out loud the names of those connected to any of us who have departed this life and gone to the Summerlands in the last turn of the Wheel of the Year or, to put it another way, in the previous twelve months.

Each festival is linked to different elements and directions, so as Samhain falls near to the element of Water, this brings the emotional feeling, the empathy of the element, into the festival. For this celebration, this is as it should be. We all have memories of our own family members and friends, as well as pets who have passed on from this life to the Summerlands. Here is a story to show how the feeling of water comes into the time in which we remember those we have known that have passed on.

A Story about Samhain

In the crowded back streets of a city in the middle of the country lived a boy who was called by the nickname 'Ashmain' or simply 'Ash'. I can't even begin to pronounce his given name; his father had come from Africa and never stayed for very long after his birth. His mum came from England and they lived with their gran in a tiny terraced house in a rundown part of the city. 'Ash' was not a name for how he looked, because he looked more like milky coffee, but his friends knew he liked to be known as 'black'. Ash had lots of friends, from his school, from folks who lived near to his home and some friends who were from the family, his cousins.

One of the biggest influences on his life had been his grandfather Bill. Ash had spent a lot of time with his granddad, sometimes talking about things, sometimes playing and often just sitting together watching a film or the TV. Granddad Bill was someone Ash could rely on to be there when he needed help with boy stuff. Bill had been in the army when he was younger and never liked to talk very much about his service years, but he did share what he had learnt about good ways to behave with others, how to look out for younger and smaller people, how to treat people with respect. The two of them had gone places together. All of his life Ash remembered doing all kinds of things with his granddad, but all that had changed now.

Granddad Bill had smoked as a young man but gave it up when Ash was a baby, because he never wanted to cause the boy any harm from his smoking. But each year as the winter had got much colder and wetter granddad had started to cough. He had one chest infection after another until he was sent to the hospital for an X-ray.

Ash remembers him getting the results of that X-ray. He had a shadow on his lungs and when they looked into that a little more they discovered he had cancer. That was four years ago and his granddad had kept going, always had a funny joke to tell his mates, never sad or even looking ill, just a little short of breath.

Ash hadn't really understood what having cancer meant at the beginning. He knew it was a serious illness. During the time granddad Bill had cancer Ash learnt that there are many types of cancer. He learnt that some types can be helped more than others, some types grow more quickly than others. Ash learnt that treatments for cancer could make you feel sick for a bit. And in the end Ash learnt that cancer is not always cured.

'Hey Ash, where's the old man?' his pals had called to him one day.

'He's gone,' said Ash. 'What do you mean?' asked his pals. 'Gone where?'

'He died,' Ash replied and went very quiet.

His pals didn't know what to say, so they slapped him on the back and said, 'He was the man, a good man.'

And with that it was accepted that his granddad had been a very good man, great to be with, knew a lot of stuff and was someone they had respect for.

That day Ash walked slowly home, he never wanted to feel like this and he just didn't know what to do or how he felt, except that he felt sad, empty. He had his head down and wasn't looking where he was going, so he walked straight into the stranger.

'Sorry mate,' said Ash as he looked up.

'That's OK,' said the man, and he looked straight at Ash, looked him in the eyes for a moment and seemed to be able to sum up the feeling coming from Ash, one of extreme sadness.

Now the man was an odd sort of a bloke, he was maybe in his twenties or a bit older. He had long hair in dreadlocks, fair dreadlocks. He wore some odd clothes, black trousers, a loose white kind of a shirt, all gathered up at the neck with long sleeves that were also gathered up into wide cuffs. He had a black waistcoat and what looked like a long dark grey jacket. Ash looked him up and down and said, 'What kind of a fashion do you call that?'

The man was not surprised or bothered by the question, 'It's Steam-Punk,' he said. 'That's what they call it now, but it's been my look for years.'

'I quite like it,' said Ash.

'Thank you,' said the man. 'But why so glum, so sad, mate?' he asked.

Ash for some reason felt he could talk to this man, and he was within sight of his house by now. 'My granddad's gone,' said Ash.

'You mean he's passed on?' said the man.

At this Ash looked him in the eye and with a little bit of anger in his voice said, 'He died, he's gone!'

The man was quiet for a moment and then he said, 'I am very sorry to hear that you have lost your granddad, that he has passed to the Summerlands, may his journey be smooth.'

'Summerlands?' said Ash, 'He went to the crem, he went up the chimney!'

'Ahh, I see you don't know where he had gone do you?'

Ash said he didn't know what the man was talking about and would he please explain, ''cause it's nearly tea time.'

'Well, you see,' said the man, 'your granddad's spirit, the bit of him that gave him his personality, his spark has left the body it was living in and travelled on to the Summerlands. It is only his overcoat so to speak that went up the chimney.'

'You mean part of him is still around?' said Ash. 'Yes,' said the man, 'and this time of year you should remember him, speak to him as you did before, think about all the great times you had together, because it's time to remember our ancestors.'

'And what is this Summerlands like?' asked Ash.

'A place that is summer all year round, with trees, flowers, all the beauty of nature, a place to rest and be happy,' the man said. 'Not everyone believes in the Summerlands, but most faiths have similar ideas of a person's spirit living on somewhere else that is good, somewhere they can be happy. People like me call it the Summerlands.'

Ash listened to this and it was if someone had turned the light on in a dark room, he understood now why his granddad had said part of him would always be with him, that he'd always watch over Ash and it made all the difference. Ash finally realized that although he'd never be able to hug his granddad again or pull funny faces with him, he could still talk to him and know that somewhere his wonderful granddad still loved him and was listening.

'Thanks for the info mate,' Ash said to the man.

'You're welcome!' said the man, and lifted his hand up for a hi-five. Ash slapped his hand in a much more positive mood now and turned to walk the last few metres to his house. Before he went in the door he turned to wave to the man.

Guess what? He'd just melted into this air, not a trace of him anywhere.

'Bye,' shouted Ash as he opened the front door, calling out to the place where he had seen the man.

'Bye Ash,' came the voice back!

And to this day Ash can't explain where the man went, he just disappeared.

A Word about Dressing Up, Trick or Treating and Halloween Parties

The history behind this is not very old, but it has become very widespread with lots of children dressing up and knocking on doors to collect sweets, apples, nuts and other treats. It is fun and I would not wish to stop anyone enjoying themselves, but it's not what the Pagan festival of Samhain, which most people call 'Halloween', is all about. Maybe it is possible to remember our ancestors, our loved ones and have a good time as well?

The children who come along to our open group do wear different things at this time of year. They come dressed as witches or wizards, perhaps other costumes and some wear dark cloaks, and they do get a few sweets, but the older children also understand what the season is all about. They know it is about remembering those who have passed on and sharing memories of them with family and friends.

So if you are going out on the night of either October 31st, or May 1st if you live in the southern hemisphere, please take care. Just visit the families who have decorated their homes with seasonal things, those that leave some clue that they don't mind you calling. Try not to frighten the grown-ups! And don't scare any babies who come to the door with their parents. If you get some sweets or some treats, remember to say thank you! And have a poem, a song or a joke ready for when the door opens.

And the tricks? Don't use anything nasty or smelly, remember you might get home to find your own home has to be cleaned up and it could possibly be your chore!

Through it all, remember those who are no longer with us in body, but can be present in spirit.

Interesting Information You Can Find and Learn about Samhain

1. All major religions have a time of the year to remember their ancestors, for Pagans it's October 31st. For established Christians it's on November 1st, which they call 'All Saints Day', followed by 'All Souls Day' on November 2nd. Jewish people remember their dead, especially those who died in the Holocaust, less than a week after Passover, which is in the spring. There are other special days when people around the world remember their ancestors, can you find them? What are they called and when are they?
(Use a notebook to answer the questions.)

2. How do other faiths remember their dead? Do they say prayers? Do they light candles? Write down in your notebook how other faiths celebrate their ancestors and loved ones who have died.

3. On the internet it is now possible to trace your own family back in most cases at least three generations. Can you do this? Perhaps you could draw a family tree and put in the names of your family going back at least three generations, that's you and any brothers or sisters you have, your parents and your grandparents. This may help you feel more of a connection with your family who came before you. If you are adopted, then why not draw a family tree of your adopted family?

4. Where did your ancestors live? In a house, a flat, a caravan or were they people who moved around and lived in different types of places?

5. These days if someone dies we either bury them or cremate their body, while their spirit leaves and travels on to the Summerlands. Do you know where your ancestors, perhaps your great great grandparents are buried or were cremated? Make a note of this in your notebook and, if you can, add a photo of the place.

6. Some faiths and cultures give gifts of some kind to their ancestors. Find out about offerings made during the Mexican Day of the Dead festival or Chinese Spirit Money.

Midwinter and Yule

The Midwinter Solstice occurs when the Sun is furthest away from where we live on the Earth and produces a very long night and a very short day. It happens in the northern hemisphere around December 20th to 23rd, the most normal date kept is December 21st. In the southern hemisphere it's between June 19th and 23rd and the best known date would be June 21st. So when Santa comes to the children in Australia they are walking around in their shirt sleeves and eating fruit salad instead of dried fruit pudding and custard!

In ancient times we are told that the wise men and women, the Shaman, or perhaps the Druid in a village would watch for this shortest day and gather the people together to watch for the Sun to be reborn, to rise again. Then, day by day as the length of daylight increased, it would herald a celebration, a feast and a holiday.

People felt that the Sun was a God, he or she was divine, powerful, and would bring the changing of the season and eventually the harvest. This God was being reborn as a tiny Sun, a child, a divine baby and they felt that the Mother Goddess was in labour all through the long night to give birth to the new baby Sun. The people would sit up all night to keep her company, they would light candles and sing songs to her and even these days there are groups who do gather together and keep vigil all through the night.

The festival occurs in the element of Earth and here we have the solid foundation for our whole year, the strength we need to build on, for without the Sun to warm the Earth and produce our food, we would be hungry. And without the solid ground to build our homes on, or even to attach our homes to, where would we be? Floating in the air? Floating in the sea or on the water?

So at this time of the year our celebration is all about homes, about gathering together and having some time off work and school to spend with our family or our friends.

Once the Sun had made a difference to the length of the days, and it took about four days to notice a difference to the amount of daylight, then a feast was held, a huge party that went on for several days. It's called 'Yule' and our ancestors would bring a huge log into the home, and in the hearth they would set fire to the middle of it. Each day the two ends would be tapped into the middle and this log would burn for the days of Yule.

So why does everyone call this time 'Christmas'? It dates back to the very early Catholic Church. The Christian Church chose to adopt the Midwinter festival and rename it, calling it at first 'Christ-Mass' and saying that the newborn 'Sun' was in fact their God who was born. Grownups who know a lot about this subject will tell you that the 'Star of Bethlehem' happened around mid-September to early October. It was in fact two planets that came into line and appeared from Earth to look like one big new star.

These early Catholics were very wise to keep the Midwinter because it is a very good idea to have a rest from work and school, to eat some good food and spend some time with our family just before the worst of the bad weather comes and we get ice and snow, which stops us from getting out and about.

A Story about Yule

Tara looked out of the window, a stray white flake of snow blew past and then it went all dark, and a mixture of rain, hail and snow blew sideways across the window outside.

'Bother,' she said to herself, 'I was going to walk to the other end of the drive and go to visit my aunt.'

Tara lived in Ireland. She lived in a little village called Doolin in county Clare. The place looked out from a rocky coastline out to sea. It was often windy there, so it was no surprise that the wind was blowing today.

Tara went to school nearby, there was a bus that collected all the children from around there and took them off to school. In the evenings, not only did she have homework to do, she played a whistle, a kind of flute that looked like a small recorder. Her aunt taught her how to play it.

Tara's Aunt Aine played in a band which got together in a pub in the village. Lots of visitors who were on holiday would come and listen. The band had a couple of folk who played the fiddle, someone who played the bodhran, a man who played a squeeze-box, which was a bit like a tiny keyboard that he strapped to his chest, and Aunt Aine who played tin whistles and flutes.

The wind dropped and suddenly the sky was clear again, so Tara took her whistle, put it in the pocket of her coat and, wrapped up against the cold wind, she left to walk down to see her aunt.

She had not gone very far when she heard music coming from the hedge by the side of the drive.

'Hello, who's there?' she asked.

'Well now, and wouldn't you like to know?' said a voice from the hedge.

'That's why I asked,' she said. 'Step out of the hedge where I can see you.'

There was a rustle of leaves and out of the hedge stepped a small man. He was not very tall.

'Hello,' said Tara. 'My name is...' and before she could get in another word the little man interrupted her.

'I know full well who you are,' he said, 'and I know where you are going and what for.'

She stood quite still and had to think very quickly. She had heard tales of small people who lived in the area; they came and went, never really lived in any house that you could see, but they would visit and talk to you if there was a good reason.

'There has to be a very good reason for you to be playing me a lovely new tune this day,' said Tara.

'Well yes,' said the man. 'It's come to our notice that you are getting very good at the music, that you practice a lot and we are thinking that it's a new tune you would be having.'

'That would be very nice, especially with Midwinter and the Yule festival coming soon, I could play it to my family and perhaps teach it to them,' said Tara.

'Now you are talking,' he said, 'and I am after teaching you this special tune to play at Midwinter.'

At that he picked up his whistle and began to play a beautiful tune. The melody was soothing and left you with a feeling of warmth, the kind of warm you feel inside yourself when you are cosy.

'That's very beautiful, and I would love to learn it,' Tara said to the man.

Then from the hedge the little man produced two three-legged stools, made of wood with turned legs; lumpy bumpy legs. They both sat down to play and within about half an hour Tara had learnt the tune and was playing it well. The man stopped playing and put his whistle down.

'You have done very well my dear, just as our folk said you would, and you must play this tune during the longest night of the year.'

'I shall,' said Tara. 'Thank you so much for teaching me. What can I do for you in return?'

'When you gather around your nice warm fire, to wait for the rebirth of the new Sun, you can invite us around your fire to share the warmth, for it gets very cold on that longest night while the Goddess is giving birth to our new light,' he said.

'But what's your name?' asked Tara. 'Who shall I call to?'

'If you just ask for those of good heart to warm themselves around your family fire, we will come,' said the little man.

With that the little man stood up, picked up the stools, walked into the hedge and, taking the stools with him, he was gone.

Tara decided not to go down to her aunt's house after all, she just went back home to write in her little notebook about her new friend and to play the music again.

Now it was her family's tradition that at Midwinter they would all gather together and entertain each other with song, story and music through the long cold night. And when Midwinter came that year, Tara stood up in front of all her family and friends and said in a loud voice, 'Will those of a good heart come and warm themselves around our family fire.' She picked up her whistle and played the new tune.

There was a bit of a rustle, and the room felt warmer. It felt as if it was full of people, but not all the family saw any of them. Some did, but only a few knew that they had special visitors.

When Tara had finished playing everyone clapped and told her how lovely that new tune was. Her Aunt Aine asked her where she had learnt it, for it was not a tune she had taught her niece. Tara smiled and looked into the shadows of the room. 'A visitor taught me,' she said. And her Aunt Aine smiled back at her knowingly and said, 'Well done!'

Everyone who could stayed up all night and greeted the daylight the next day. They had a hot drink and then most of them went off to bed for a sleep. One or two of the youngest members of the family had already fallen asleep by the fire during the darkness, lulled by the songs and stories played and told in the night.

Tara said, 'Good morning good folk, welcome to the light.' Her friend who had taught her the special tune stepped out of the shadow of the room, lifted his hat and said, 'Welcome indeed, blessings on all of you!' And with that he was off.

Where did he go? You should ask the folks who meet in the pub in the village of Doolin, someone will perhaps know who he was and where he and his family lived. I promised not to tell, 'the gentry' would be very cross with me if I did tell you.

Interesting Information You Can Find and Learn about Midwinter and Yule

1. We have a celebration, a family party four days after the Winter Solstice and we Pagans call this 'Yule'. Other faiths also have a winter celebration and the best known one is 'Christ-Mass' now known as Christmas. Can you find out how many other faiths have a winter celebration? What do they call it? Write your answers in your notebook.

2. At midwinter we make a drink with spices and either red wine or redcurrant juice. We drink this warm, what is it called? The Germans have a special name for this hot winter drink, can you find out what this is called?

3. At this time of year we have less daylight. Can you keep a note of the time it becomes daylight and the time it gets dark for three days after the Midwinter Solstice? When the length of daylight gets longer, we can start the celebration of Yule. (Keep a note of this in your book.)

4. Santa Claus is a story that comes from another country. Can you find out which country the story comes from? When do you think the well known Santa was painted with red and white clothes? Who started this red and white Santa?

5. Long ago boxes were given by the Lord of the Manor to his servants and to the poor of his village. These had little presents in them. This happened the day after 'Christ-Mass', which Pagans call 'Yule'. What is the day after Christmas day called now in modern times?

Imbolc

By the time Imbolc arrives on Feb 1st in the northern hemisphere and August 1st in the southern hemisphere, the Wheel has turned a little away from the Earth element and is now being influenced a little by the Air element. The ground is still solid in most places, frozen by the cold winter and yet in the topsoil, perhaps pushing through snow or ice, snowdrops are making an appearance. There are so many different varieties of this white flower with its fine lines of green, some with double or even triple inner petals that look like a ballet dress for a fairy. It's a sure sign that spring will arrive eventually.

Many festivals can be linked to different deities, but this one is Brigit's festival. She is a Celtic Irish Goddess who has been so popular that when Christianity came to these shores the early Roman Catholic Church simply called her a saint and kept her feast day. She is often referred to as 'the Mary of the Gaels'. I am sure that you already know a great deal about her, but let's just go over a few brief points to refresh your memory.

According to ancient Irish stories, she was the daughter of the Dagda, the Good God. She had two sisters of the same age, both also called Brigit and she governs the hearth, the blacksmith and metalcraft; healing, especially midwifery; poetry and prose. Some see her as a triple Goddess while others see her as a single Goddess with many different gifts.

The word 'Imbolc' means 'first milk' and it is at this time that the ewes start to get their first milk ready for their lambs, which will be born over the next few weeks.

In many Pagan groups, Wiccan, Druid and Druidcraft, Imbolc is a traditional time for new beginnings and as a fire festival it's an ideal chance to write down on a piece of paper the goals you wish to reach this summer. These can be burnt on a little bonfire , or simply in a fireproof bowl.

When we think of the Goddess Brigit at this time of the year we see her as a maiden, an unmarried young woman or a woman who has not had any children. So we often see her dressed in white, often with a circlet of white flowers on her head. She carries a candle or has a small fire and around her are lambs. In my humble opinion it is not until later in the year that we see her as a full-blooded Fire Goddess, watching over the blacksmith, and by then she will be far more mature and be wearing passionate red.

This is a very lovely festival for young people. A simple way of expressing this would be to turn all the lights out and then light one candle, and from that one candle everyone can light a candle. The clear pure white light which fills the space, growing from one tiny light, is very much like the first breath and the new life that each and every living thing will experience.

A Story about Imbolc

Declan was his mum's right-hand man. He was the one who put the bins out, put new washers on the bathroom taps, oiled the door hinges so the door didn't creak and squeak like something out of a mystery movie. In fact in the last year since his dad had left, he had been the very best support his mum could have wanted. His little sister was eight now and she did do her best to help about the house too, but she wasn't very tall or very strong for that matter.

Declan's mum Joyce had thought she was happily married, but out of the blue her husband left with a younger women and went to live in Spain. It came as a great shock to the rest of the family. His mum and dad had seemed to be getting on well, they never had any terrible rows, but on the other hand they never seemed to be all that close either, so maybe they just fell out of love?

The family had never been very religious, the children had gone along to church with the school as everyone else did, but it never did register much, and the stories that some of his pals told him about other schools, well they were far worse. At least his school only took them into church twice a year and had the vicar came in from time to time to the assembly. But just over the last few months Joyce had started to go along to some outdoor Druid meetings.

Now Declan loved the outdoors, in fact he spent his spare time helping the farmer who had a flock of sheep on the outskirts of the town. If he went up on a Saturday early he could go out on a quad bike with the farmer and check the sheep, make sure the silly creatures had not got themselves stuck in a fence, or fallen into a stream. The sheep were getting big as they had put the rams to the flock about five months ago and those chaps had done their work and covered all the ewes, so hopefully they were all pregnant.

It was the last week in January and it had been very cold, but the weather had warmed up just a little over the last few days. With luck the last of winter was behind them now.

When Saturday came Declan got up early, got dressed and had his breakfast, tiptoed in to see his mum who was still very sleepy and kissed her goodbye. He put his boots and coat on and left for the farm.

He found the farmer a bit on edge. There had been a fox calling in the night and this would make the sheep restless. So close to lambing, that could be dangerous. The pair of them mounted the quad bikes and drove across the fields to check the sheep. They were unharmed, yet it was clear that they were fidgety, and the farmer said he was not sure if they were starting to lamb or if the fox had got them in a state. If they lambed too early the little ones would not be strong enough to survive.

Declan spent the day with the farmer. They took extra feed out to the sheep, checked the fence for any holes, spent about an hour walking through the flock and talking to them, checking them and the farmer showed Declan how to check if the pregnant ewes were coming into milk.

'Look,' he said, 'all you do is hold the teat between your first finger and your thumb and squeeze gently and pull very slightly at the same time, not too hard. If she's almost ready you will get a small amount of cloudy thick milk out.' It took Declan a few times to get it right, but soon he got the hang of it. He and the farmer worked their way right through the flock and sprayed a mark on the backs of the sheep who were close to lambing.

He had a good lunch in the farmhouse. The farmer's wife produced a huge saucepan of what she called soup, but it was far more like a stew, full of vegetables, pulses, little dumplings and chunks of ham. This was washed down with a cup of tea. Then, after a break for about half an hour, the two of them went back out to take some hay to the sheep and a block of minerals which the farmer just called, 'a lick'. It was a large square solid thing that they put into a plastic container and as soon as they got it in place the sheep were pushing around it to have a lick.

By about tea time it was getting dark. Declan had a cup of tea and a very nice piece of fruit cake at the farm and then went home.

Once back at his home he started to tell his mum all about the fox who was worrying the sheep, the size of them and that they were close to lambing.

'The farmer's very worried,' he told Joyce, 'if the fox comes back and makes more trouble the ewes could go into labour early and the lambs would be too small and die.'

Joyce listened intently to the story and then checked her watch, but not for the time, she was looking at the date.

'I have an idea that might help,' she said. Declan couldn't think what his mum could possibly do to help. He'd really only told her all about the sheep because he knew she was lonely and was interested in what he had been doing. Not all his pals talked to their parents in this way, he knew that, but in the year since his dad had taken off with another woman, Declan had got to know his mum as a friend and they chatted quite a bit.

Joyce had gone off into the kitchen and came back with a little white candle. She put it into a candleholder on the shelf above the fire place and lit it.

'This is for your sheep, I'm asking Brigit to help keep them safe,' she said.

Declan looked at the candle and at his mum. Something inside him warned him not to laugh, not to upset her, after all what harm could a simple candle do?

The next day was Sunday. Declan went back to the farm for half a day, just to help with the extra feeding for the flock. The farmer left his dogs back at the farmhouse. He didn't want the dogs upsetting the sheep either, so they set off with a little trailer hitched to the back of one of the quad bikes and went down into the fields.

When they got to the field they found a young woman drawing pictures of the sheep, she had long red hair and was wearing very warm clothes and fingerless gloves.

'I hope you don't mind, but it's such a peaceful scene that I just had to stop and draw the sheep,' said the woman.

'That's all right, so long as you don't go wandering around inside the field,' said the farmer.

'I won't,' said the young woman and she went back to her drawing of the sheep who were very peaceful, happily chewing away, munching on the grass.

Declan and the farmer left the extra feed for the sheep, walked through the flock and checked them all, made sure they had water and then went back to the farm for tea.

They were sitting eating a second piece of a very nice fruit cake when the door knocker went, and the farmer's wife went off to answer it. She came back with a little white card, like a business card in her hand.

'Who was it love?' asked the farmer.

'She said she was an artist and she has been drawing the sheep, and also that she would be back to do more over the next few days.'

'That's fine,' said the farmer. 'She seems to have very peaceful vibes and the sheep like her.'

Then he looked down at the card, expecting to find a phone number or a web site address, but no, in fact there was only one word on the card, it was a name, 'Brigit'.

'Brigit, did you say?' asked Declan.

'Here, you can have the card if you like, take it home to show your mum.' Declan looked down at the card, then put it into his pocket without a word.

A little later Declan was standing in his sitting room at home telling Joyce all about his time on the farm and about the artist. 'Here, have the card, the farmer told me to show it to you,' he said.

Joyce took the card and looked down at it, then her face drained of all colour for a moment. 'I told you she would help, look at the name,' she said. 'It's Brigit. She's sent someone to keep an extra eye on the sheep!'

And both of them just looked at the card and then at each other, then they went and found another candle and lit it. Both of them said together, 'For Brigit, to help with the lambs.'

Several months later, when the days were long and the lambs were almost as tall as their mums, the farmer had a delivery; he wasn't expecting it at all. It was a painting of his sheep in the field and it was simply signed 'Brigit'.

Declan has a copy, framed in his bedroom now, and it's started a whole new subject for them all to look into, it all started at Imbolc, when Brigit came to draw a picture.

Interesting Information You Can Find and Learn about Imbolc

1. Imbolc is the time of year when we can see the very first early signs of spring. What flowers can you see at this time of year in your area? Are there other plants that show early signs of spring in your area?

2. Mother sheep are called 'ewes' and they have their lambs in the spring time. If you have any farms with sheep near you, try to find out when the lambing starts in your area. What other animals usually give birth in the spring? Can you find out what animal gives birth the earliest in your area?

3. There is a special Goddess we associate with this time of the year, she is called 'Brigit' or 'Bridget' and she was said to love animals, healing sick ones and helping the ewes give birth to the lambs. Where did she come from? Can you find out more about her?

4. Many Pagans think of our Goddess as being a Maiden, a Mother and a Wise Woman. Can you find out which aspect of the Goddess we celebrate at this time of year? Is it Maiden, Mother, or Wise Woman?

5. There is a drink, a liquid which is connected to this time of year, what is it? How many different types of this drink have you tried? If you have never tried this drink or only one type and you are not allergic to it perhaps your parents will help you get some different types of this drink to taste.

Again, when you find your answers write them in your notebook, if you can add pictures to your notes this will be even better.

Ostara, Spring Equinox

Having first looked at the elements from a Pagan point of view, we are now placing those elements onto the Wheel of the Year and learning how the element itself influences the season. The festival of the Spring Equinox is linked in the East here in Europe and is linked to the element of Air.

In the northern hemisphere the Spring Equinox or Ostara is between March 19th to 23rd, while in the southern hemisphere it falls between September 19th to 23rd.

It's a time of equal day and night as the word 'equinox' suggests, everything is in balance, poised to burst into action. This is the start of the Sun's progress through the Zodiac belt and begins at 0° of Aries.

The Air element connects with the wind, it also brings us clear thought, fast mental ability. This is the ability to think a situation out in order to come to a clear understanding of a problem, and it is the essence that it brings to the festival of Ostara.

The name Ostara is from the Anglo-Saxon Goddess of the spring, Eostara or Ostara. She was said to bring the spring with her on a fresh new breeze. She is often depicted with baby animals and surrounded with flowers, spring flowers which, on the whole, come from bulbs.

So the Air element blows into the year, bringing with it a sense of balance, and at the head is the Goddess Ostara. By now, with equal day and equal night, there are enough light hours that chickens have come fully into lay, meaning most domestic hens will lay an egg each day. We can afford now to have them boiled, scrambled, fried, made into an omelette and used in cakes and puddings. Bright painted and hard boiled eggs, dyed with food colours, are associated with this festival.

March is also the month when hares pair up in order to mate and have their offspring, which are called 'leverets'. Hares have very long back legs. They can stand up on their back legs and will race and chase each other, standing up to have elaborate boxing matches. The hare is very much associated with Ostara and in very early days people thought that the hare laid eggs! This strange idea came about because once the baby leverets had left the nest, which was simply a hollowed out area in open grassland, ground laying birds would take the nest over. The nest was already lined with soft underfur that the female hare had pulled out of her coat to form a warm, comfortable bed for her babies. This provided ready-made warmth and comfort for the birds to lay their eggs on and raise their own babies.

You can see that the name 'Easter' has been taken from the Anglo-Saxon Goddess of the spring and given to the Christian celebration which comes three days after the Jewish Passover. Because this is a Moon Festival, Easter itself changes from year to year whereas our 'Ostara' remains constant and is timed when the Sun begins its journey through the Zodiac belt and the day and night are of equal length. Many of the Pagan customs, especially the connection to eggs, have been taken on and almost before we take Christmas decorations down the Easter eggs start to appear in the shops. It has become a very commercial holiday with chocolate eggs, cards and now decorations.

A Story about Ostara

Half term had lasted only four days, or seven if you wanted to count the weekend. And now, back to school after the break, Irá was working towards a project about where our food comes from. She was one of only a few non-Catholic children in her school. The rest of her class had to have lessons about their faith and 'doctrine' regarding being a Roman Catholic. This was fine because it meant that Irá was able to take on different subjects and this term, as it headed towards the spring break, she was learning about farming and land management. This meant going off into the countryside at the weekend or during a day off and finding out why farmers had fields that they never planted some years and never used to graze animals either. These fields were laid fallow, rested and left for nature.

Irá had come out to a particular farm about four times now, just to take photos and draw, make notes about what animals were to be found and what the farmer used his fields for. It was a great surprise to see lots of hares racing around the fallow field, and then stopping and turning to face each other and box! It was a wonderful sight and Irá took some photos for her project.

It was a clear day, only a few wisps of cloud high up in the sky, the bright spring sunshine lighting up the countryside, which meant you could see for miles and miles.

She wasn't alone, she was there with her Uncle John, her mum's brother who himself was a very keen photographer, so today was a very good day for both of them.

'Just look at them run,' Irá said to her Uncle. 'There's one on its own at the far end of the field'.

'So there is,' said Uncle John. 'Let's walk down the lane and see if we can see where it's going.'

So they walked down the lane alongside the field to the far end to observe the lone hare. It was a female and she spotted them as they walked along. She stood very still for a while and just watched, her nose twitching. Then she ran towards a gap in the hedge. By the time Irá and her Uncle had reached the end of the field, they could see the lane had a little path leading off which followed the top of the field. They could hear a scream, a strange sound, and it seemed to come from the path.

'Listen, is that an animal?' asked Irá.

'I don't know, but whoever or whatever it is seems to be in great pain, let's see if we can help at all,' her Uncle said.

Uncle John put his camera into its bag and put the bag on his back. Irá also put her camera away in her pocket and together they walked fast towards the scream. As they had walked towards the corner of the field they had lost sight of the hare and as they turned onto the path, about two metres along it was a woman lying on the ground, clutching her leg.

The woman was not very old, she looked as if she was around thirty. She had long brown hair which was loose, falling down her back, and she wore what looked like a long dark dress with a belt in the middle; strange clothes for countryside. You saw most people in jeans or trousers and T-shirts and jumpers, not many would even consider wearing a dress in the country.

'Help me please,' said the woman. 'I fell. I think I caught my leg on something and it's cut and twisted.' They looked down at her leg as she lay on the ground. Both of them could see bleeding and noticed that her ankle was at an odd angle.

'We can help you as best we can, but I think we need to phone for the emergency services, I think you will need to go to the hospital to get that ankle fixed,' Uncle John said.

'No, just help me to stop the bleeding and give me a hand home,' the woman said. She seemed to be very worried at the idea of a hospital.

Irá and her uncle worked, wrapping a bandage with a pad under it around the woman's leg. They managed to stop the bleeding, but still the woman didn't want them to send for outside help. She said all she needed was a hand to get home, that it was just a strain and she could manage it herself once she was home.

'If you are absolutely sure, then of course we can help you back to your home,' said Uncle John, and then he and Irá supported the woman on both sides and walked her down the path to her little house, which was more like a cottage, a bit further down the path.

It was a strange place, it was like stepping back in time. There were piles of logs outside her back door and a large sturdy looking broom made of twigs tied to a straight branch propped up. It was the kind of brush Irá had seen in the garden centre she visited with her mum.

They helped the woman inside to her kitchen, which had bunches of what looked like herbs handing from the ceiling on a very old fashioned wooden drying rack.

They settled the woman down on a chair in the kitchen and asked again if they could send for someone to help her.

'No, I'll be just fine now,' said the woman. 'Your quick action has stopped the bleeding and I shall be able to deal with this ankle myself.'

They turned to go but the women called out to stop them. 'I must give you something for helping me,' she said and reached over to the table where a box with some eggs was sitting. 'Here, take these eggs, my hens laid them this week, I want you to have them.'

Irá and her uncle thanked the woman, left the cottage and walked back down the path where they turned along the lane to go back to where their car was parked at the other end of the fallow field.

As they got near to the car, Uncle John turned to Irá and said, 'Just one more photo before we go home.' He took his camera out of his bag.

Irá took her camera out of her pocket and both turned around to take just one more photo.

At the far end of the field was a movement and a hare came into view, they both went to focus their cameras and then it moved again and they took a sharp breath.

'Look uncle,' said Irá, 'that hare has a bandage on one of her back legs!'

Shocked they put the cameras down and looked at each other and back at the field.

The hare with a bandage was carrying something in her mouth and running back the way she had come, it was a tiny baby hare.

'She's got young,' said Uncle John and they both watched as the hare disappeared through the hedge and back in the direction of the woman's cottage.

Interesting Information You Can Find and Learn about the Spring Equinox

1. The length of day and night are equal at this time of the year. What time does it get light and what time does it get too dark to see for driving? (This is known as 'lighting up time' and is when our parents, teachers and guardians have to put on the lights on their cars on to drive.) Keep a note of these times for three days.

2. Find out more about the astronomy of equinoxes by looking them up on the internet or in a library.

3. The Anglo Saxon Goddess who was said to bring the spring is called 'Ostara'. Which country did she come from?

4. The hare is very special to Pagans and is connected to this celebration. Where do hares have their babies and what are they called? Find out if there is anywhere near you where you can see hares in the wild. If you want to find out more about hares, try looking them up on the internet or in a library.

5. The egg is also linked to this time of year, why do you think this is? (Find out and write the answer in your notebook.)

6. We celebrate the arrival of spring at this time of year and we give children chocolate eggs. Christians also give eggs in the spring time, but not at Ostara, when do Christians give eggs to their children? Do you know of any other faith that gives sweets or chocolate to children at special festivals in the year? In your notebook, make a note of which other faiths do this and when.

Beltane

Moving away from the element of Air now and going towards the element of Fire, we reach the next point on the Wheel of the Year, which is Beltane. This is a fire festival and one of the best known festivals of the Pagan year. The feeling here is one of passion, of energy, but still with an amount of Air, so we get quick mentality along with the fierce passion. Beltane is the celebration of the marriage or the joining of the Goddess to the God.

Paganism is a fertility religion, the spark of magical energy that occurs when both masculine and feminine energies meet in order to create. I say this so many times to people while I am taking a ceremony, this is not only about the physical joining that humans undertake in order to create a new life, this is also about the creation of animals, crops, poetry, prose and artwork of all kinds.

There are differences between the various paths within the overall Pagan group. For instance, Wicca will celebrate the joining of the Goddess to the God and they do this often symbolically by the use of a chalice (cup) for the female and the athame (knife) for the male. It's that magical moment when the flow of positive and negative combine to produce something unique and different.

There is a great deal of talk and gossip about this joining rite, spoken about in Witchcraft circles as 'the great rite', the actual joining of Goddess, represented by a High Priestess, and God, represented by a High Priest. I can tell you that many Wiccan couples who run groups and covens are also couples in life, and many will conduct their own rites, celebrations together in the privacy of their own home. It's not something that any Wiccan would speak about to others outside their group. Each rite is carried out in a circle, and what goes on inside the circle is up to the people present and no-one else. Usually you would need to be a full adult to become an active member of a Wiccan group or coven. Some Wiccan groups may organise festivals and celebrations that non-members and children can be invited to and these would be a bit different to the rites of an adult group.

However, Druidcraft, which is a blend of both Druidry and Wicca, does not have such hard and fast rules. Provided a parent or guardian of a young person is with them, someone of any age can come along to one of these celebrations.

Druidcraft on the whole has meetings and celebrations outdoors, under the sky, as do most Druid groups.

Druidry celebrates the product of that joining of energies, what is created. That could be a child or it could be a work of art or a magical healing. Druids often speak of the 'Awen' the flow of universal energy which is called upon, sung, written about and sent out into the world as energy, most of the time healing energy.

There are so many other Pagan paths, including Shamanism, where individuals work with spirits of animals, plants and ancestors, or Heathens who worship the Scandinavian and Germanic Gods and have rituals based on what is known of the Heathen practices that people like the Vikings followed.

Just as each person is unique, even within identical twins scientists have found differences, no two Pagan paths are exactly alike. Not any one Pagan path is right for everyone, and yet there are enough similarities between the paths that groups of people can gather together, work, celebrate and worship together.

Beltane is a festival that many will be drawn to, folks of different paths, Wiccans, Druids, Shamans and many others. Although Heathens do have their own festivals, many will also come along and celebrate Beltane.

A Story about Beltane

'Talbern, have you finished your chores yet?' asked his mother.

'That's the last one done, now can I go off to meet the gang?' he asked. His mother said yes, so at last, having done all his chores Talbern could go off and meet up with the planning group, the gang who were going to organise the pageant and fire for Beltane this year.

It was something that was put on every year; a great bonfire and a group of people from all the little towns in the area getting together, all dressed up as some aspect of Beltane.

When he got to the meeting it was almost over, the gang had made their minds up about what their group would be and who was going to be which character.

'So what did you decide?' asked Talbern. The answer was not exactly what he had thought, especially as he wasn't there when they all made their minds up.

'You are going to be Herne,' said one of the boys, 'and we are all going to be dressed as the green man so when we all stand together we are going to look like a forest.'

That would mean that Talbern would have to wear a headdress with antlers, and very little else, maybe shorts covered in a fur, to make him look very shamanic.

'I don't know the first thing about this character Herne,' said Talbern, 'but I guess I shall just have to do some research and come up with the character.'

The meeting broke up soon after that. Talbern had been late because he'd had to catch up with his chores that he never did during the week. If he wanted any time to himself at the weekend, he knew that he would have to get to grips with his boring chores during the week.

Talbern lived in a small town in America, and he was now towards the end of the sixth grade. After the summer vacation he would go into the final year of the middle school. He was twelve years old and he was well grown for his years, looking more like a teenager. But Talbern was not as mature as a teenager, he'd never had a girlfriend, in fact the thought never came into his head. Many of his pals had girlfriends, but although he got on very well with the girls in his year, none of them were 'special' to him. He spent his spare time either playing games on his computer, or he kept his mum company when she went off on walks. Talbern loved the out of doors, he liked walking through the forests with his mum, and when they did go on vacation they would go camping and walk during the days, stopping by lakes and go wild swimming in the water. He was a suntanned, strong looking boy. I guess he came from an 'unconventional' family.

Talbern soon got his chores under control during the weeks that led up to Beltane.

He had to deal with all the trash, and sort out the recycling. He had to keep his own room clean, which included washing the window so he could actually see out of it! His mum got the groceries on her way home from work, but it was his job to lift them all out of the car and into the kitchen. His chores were very much like all other kids' chores, most likely all over the world.

That left the weekend free for him to go into town and meet up with the gang who were doing the Beltane pageant. They had worked hard on the costumes, the masks and the headdress and all was getting ready.

'The girls' group are organising the Goddess parts for the pageant,' said one of his friends at the gang meeting just the week before Beltane.

'I never knew what the girls were doing. Does it make any difference to us?' asked Talbern.

'Only to you, you have to go on the float with one of them and just look cool!'

Bit by bit the story came out, no wonder they had chosen him while he wasn't there to defend himself! Not only did he have to wear a pair of antlers for the day, he now had to stand with some girl and look 'cool' and be her partner. Oh well, it could have been worse, it could have been little girls in fairy costumes, at least this was someone his own age group and perhaps he may even know her.

This year, Beltane was a Saturday and the whole event was timed to end with a big bonfire on rough ground on the outskirts of the town. There would be plenty of folks there, no doubt the whole town would turn out and just have fun.

The float turned out to be a big truck, decorated to look like a wood, with trees and artificial grass. Talbern was ready before it kicked off and all his pals turned up on time, all dressed in their costumes. They looked great and, if they all stood together very still, it just looked like a wood.

The girls' gang turned up on time as well, they were all dressed as priestesses with long robes tied in the middle with cords, belts made of different strands of silk curtain cord, and they all looked great. Then Talbern spotted the one chosen for the main role. He froze. He'd never actually seen a better looking girl. She had very long loose fair hair and she had a robe which was in two halves. The top was like a swimming costume which had been draped in gold chains, thin long chains. The bottom of her costume looked like transparent red material which came from a gold belt around her hips leaving her middle bare.

He pulled himself together and realised that this role he had to play for today was going to be very nice indeed, much nicer than he had ever thought.

He went over and introduced himself to her and she smiled and fluttered her eyelashes at him. This was a whole new ball game!

What more can I tell you? The girls name was Dana, her grandparents were of Irish descent and she was well into Celtic stuff. She was in the same grade and like him was well grown for her age, looking more like a very beautiful teenager.

They got on great that day, and he protected her from all the other guys and from some of the folks who came along to see the event. In fact he stayed with her all evening as well, hardly left her side and as far as I know, they are still seeing a lot of each other, Talbern and Dana. I guess they are just right for each other.

Interesting Information You Can Find and Learn about Beltane

1. We celebrate the joining of the God with the Goddess at this time of year. What is the name often given to the pagan wedding ceremony which joins two people in love?

2. The festival falls on the Wheel of the Year between the element of Air, which we think of as yellow, and the element of Fire which we think of as red. Paint or draw a Beltane picture using these colours. What other colours do you see in the world around you at this time of year?

3. Beltane is very much a festival of love. Which flower would you associate with love? Where does this flower come from? A tree? A bush? A bulb? Find or take a photo of a flower you think is associated with love.

4. Wiccans celebrate the joining of the God and Goddess; Druids go one step on from there, what do they celebrate or think of at this time of year?

5. In Scotland, UK, there is a well known fire festival at Beltane in Edinburgh. Try to find out what happened in areas of Scotland and Wales with livestock at this time of the year. Did Fire play a special part in what happened?

Midsummer

Next on the Wheel of the Year comes Midsummer, which in the northern hemisphere happens around 19th to the 23rd of June and in the southern hemisphere between 19th and 23rd December. So while we in Britain are basking in sunshine and about to finish school for the summer Holidays, over on the other side of the world they are in the middle of their winter

In the middle of summer the day is at its longest and the night is very short, further north in Europe they don't have any dark night, eventually it gets close to dusk and within an hour is dawn again.

Midsummer is connected with the Fire element and we have already talked a little about the manner in which this passion, energy and heat can affect us. It's even possible that the strength of the Fire element can make us aggressive, angry, close to a fight. The wheel has turned now too far away from the Air element for us to have a great deal of thought and not far enough for us to feel the empathy of Water. It's full-on energy and passion.

The Sun has been beating down now for weeks, and the rain has also come and our crops are growing in the fields. Within weeks they will be ready to harvest.

This is a solar festival, and it's well known that in England hundreds gather at Stonehenge to watch the Sun rise on the longest day. This in itself is a little strange because modern scientists have discovered that Stonehenge is aligned to the Mid-winter Solstice and was a memorial ground. They have discovered many graves in and around the stone circle so it would seem that this very famous megalithic monument has something to do with death and rebirth, and may in fact be an ancient graveyard.

It is said in some mythologies that a great horse pulls the Sun across the sky, drawn in a mighty chariot. You can just imagine a fierce Sun God standing on his chariot, wielding a sword all ready to fight.

In our ceremonies we often call to a Stag at the Fire element in a circle and talk about *the Stag in the heat of the chase,* and what this refers to is the way in which the Stag comes into his own. When the deer are in rut, needing to be mated, the Stag is overcome with this great need, he fights to gain control of his herd, he is full of passion. He eats very little, drinks just a small amount, he only has one thing on his mind and that is to mate with his herd.

This is the effect that the element of Fire has on the Stag and that amount of passion can also touch us at Midsummer. We can be full of energy, or so over-full of energy that it makes us angry and want to fight!

A Story about Midsummer

If you had ever met or known a tomboy, a girl who is unlike other girls, someone who's not interested in dances, parties or clothes, then you would understand where Rife was coming from. While other girls were playing with dolls, she was racing toy cars across the room. When it came to clothes, most girls of her age would be wanting to keep up with fashion, have all the latest colours, the latest hair style, but not Rife. She never cared about clothes, she never wore a skirt or a dress. Every time you saw her she was dressed in jeans and a T-shirt. She only wore trainers or boots, and she had her hair cut short, almost as short as a boy's hair. It was copper red, and when she was trying to concentrate on something she would rub her hand backwards through her hair, which would make it stand up on end. You could have been mistaken for thinking she was a boy, and perhaps she wished she had been born a boy? Rife was an only child, both her parents worked full-time. Her dad was a chemist who worked for a company that made pills. Her mum was a teacher, so there were good wages coming into the family, Rife could have had clothes, shoes, all kinds of things, but she just wasn't interested.

Each weekday morning her parents would have their brief breakfast, leave the table with some of the breakfast things on it and go off to work, calling to Rife on their way out, 'See you later dear, have a good day,' they would call. And they would get the reply, 'Yep, later!' and the house went quiet. Rife would hurry into her clothes, run a comb through her hair without even looking in a mirror and run down the stairs two at a time.

About then the postman would shove the post through the letter box and she would go and collect it and look through the envelopes to see if there was anything at all for her or indeed anything for just anyone. A glossy leaflet said in large letters 'Urban Fox Cull' and details about the plans of the local council to trap and kill the fox population in and around where they lived. There were lots of leaflets and a letter asking the house holder to put all these through the doors of neighbour's homes.

How could they do such a thing? Do these stupid people have no understanding about the balance of nature? Rife was so angry! She wanted to tear all these leaflets up, but that was not good enough she thought.

She looked out of her kitchen window and all at once she made her mind up. She cared deeply about nature and loved foxes, so she would burn all of these. She never stopped to think about any of this, she picked up a box of matches and the pile of leaflets and went into the garden. By the side of the shed was a metal bin used for burning, she put all the leaflets in the bin and set fire to them, striking a match and dropping it alight into the middle of the paper.

Whoosh! It caught very quickly and the flames climbed higher and higher, as they leapt up they licked the side of the shed with red and yellow flames. Then it happened, the edge of the shed caught fire and started to crackle, and at first Rife never moved a muscle, still angry about the local council and their plans to cull the foxes.

Crackle, crackle and then a big crack and huge flames jumped into the air, something inside the shed had caught fire and was burning strongly. In that split second after the huge 'crack' sound Rife knew she was in trouble, she did the wrong thing, the metal bin was far too close to the garden shed.

Rife ran into the house and picked up the phone and dialled...999, a calm voice on the other end asked, 'Emergency service, which service do you require, Fire, Police or Ambulance?'

'Fire, quickly please,' said Rife and she waited for what seemed like ages but was in fact only a few seconds before a man's calm voice said at the other end, 'Fire service, can you tell me who you are and where the problem is?' Rife answered and told the man where she was, and where the fire was and then had to answer questions about her name and age. While the man at the other end of the Fire Service was talking to her she could hear the sirens of a fire engine in the distance. The man was telling her to stay away from the shed, not to go near it, that they would be with her very quickly.

She put the phone down and ran back out to the garden, the whole shed was a blaze, flames licking the wooden fence behind the shed and clouds of dense black smoke. She remembered that her dad kept his grass cutter and all the fuel for it inside the shed and she realized this was what had caught.

By the time the fire engine arrived she was shaking, her face ashen, all colour drained from her face and her eyes were wide open like dark green pools. Her face was dirty from the smoke and this made her look even more grey, both the lack of colour in her face and the effect of all the smoke.

The firemen had the fire under control very quickly and the fireman in charge of the crew came over and asked where her parents were. 'They went to work,' she said.

'I need their names and phone numbers at work please,' said the fireman.

Rife went into the house and found her notebook where she had all the phone numbers of everyone she needed to keep in touch with, parents, the school and some of her best friends. 'Here you are, this is it,' she said.

The fireman phoned with his own mobile phone and was quickly talking to Rife's dad. 'I think you had better come home, there has been a fire, no one is hurt, just shocked.' From the look on the man's face she could almost guess what her dad was saying. The man turned his phone off, turned to Rife and said, 'Your father is on his way home, and your mother too, I think it would be best if you just sat down and waited for them.'

About ten minutes later her parents found her sitting on a chair in the kitchen shaking from head to foot, still ashen grey and instead of telling her off her mum just held her close and kept saying, 'You're all right, no one is hurt, it was only a shed, it can be replaced,' and Rife guessed who would be making the new shed and that, when the whole story came out, she would no doubt be grounded for a long time!

A few months later

Rife and her parents stood back and looked at the new shed, and the new fence behind the shed, and they were all very pleased with their work. Rife herself had learnt a big lesson, to count to ten when she got angry. Her dad had been out and bought a shredder and now all the leaflets that were not needed or indeed even wanted were shredded.

And the fox cull? There was a lot of cover about the story in the local newspaper and online, in the local Facebook group, word spread very quickly that a young girl had been so upset about the idea she had set fire to her parents shed. There was a huge movement against the cull, the local MP was involved and the end result was to stop the terrible cull taking place!

But I don't for one moment suggest it was a good idea to set fire to those leaflets. Fire is very powerful and can destroy things. Yes, new things came out of it, but do you think it was a good idea in the first place?

Interesting Information You Can Find and Learn about Midsummer

1. The element for this time of year is Fire and we think of the heat of the Sun. How long is the length of day at this time of year? Make a note of when it becomes light and when it becomes dark at this time of year. (If you live in a far north part of the world, then make a note of when you start to see a little dark during the twenty-four hours.)

2. Which colour is associated with this element? And what direction is associated with Fire for you, where you live?

3. Druids are well known for gathering together to celebrate the Midsummer sunrise, but where is the most well-known place where they do this? What was this place probably used for by our ancestors? If you know then write the answer in your notebook.

4. Midsummer is also known as another name, what is it? There are two of these in the year, what would the other one be called? When would the other one be? Draw a circle in your notebook and mark when these two celebrations take place.

5. In early myths it was said that an animal pulled the Sun across the sky. Which animal was this? Can you draw or photograph one of these and put it into your notebook?

6. There is a play written about Midsummer by a very famous playwright. Can you find out what it is called and something about the story in the play?

Lughnasadh

Once again the wheel turns and moves away from the element of Fire and starts to move towards Water. It's now half way between the two and both elements have an effect on the season and on the festival. Lughnasadh or Lammas is celebrated in the northern hemisphere on August 1st and in the southern hemisphere on February 1st. It is the grain/corn/bread festival and the first Harvest Festival.

There are myths and ancient stories about the Corn King having grown to full adulthood and giving his life to feed his people. The Mother Goddess allows the 'killing' of the Corn King in order for him to grow again next year. In some places a play is performed, enacting the story of the love the Goddess has for her God and even though she loves him, she will have him put to death for the sake of her children.

The harvest takes place and the corn or the grain is collected by the farmer in order to be milled, ground into flour to make bread. Some of the grain is saved to be sown back into the fields next year and, in this way, the cycle will continue to feed the people.

For our ceremony we make some bread, perhaps braid the dough and then cook it into a large loaf. We bless this during our ceremony and then share it with everyone present, giving some to the fairy folk and some to nature for the little animals. Pagan folk have three Harvest Festivals; the first is the grain or corn harvest, then comes the apple harvest and last of all there is a berry harvest. But of all of them, it's this first one most people will remember and celebrate.

Lugh is the Celtic Sun God who gives his name to this time of year. He held a gathering with games, just like the Olympic games, when the person who won the contest was held in very high esteem. Lugh did this to honour the death of his own foster mother, the goddess Tailtiu, who worked herself to death to clear the plains for agriculture.

The Anglo-Saxons also celebrated this festival and called it 'Loaf-Mass'.

In fact all over Europe and in Canada and America this time of year is Harvest Festival time.

Because Lughnasadh is still being strongly affected by the element of Fire, it gives us a great deal of passion and energy. Red is the colour you would wear at this time. At the same time the element of Water, which governs feelings, emotions and empathy, is starting to touch the celebration and we feel the grief of the Goddess who has to sacrifice her Corn King in order to feed her children. It's very sad to see fields and fields of cut grain, all with their heads cut off leaving yellow stalks. It is even worse when the farmers come to harvest all the stalks and bale them into straw, ready to use as winter bedding or to give for extra animal feed.

There was an old tradition that allowed those who lived near the farms to go and collect the odd corn which was growing at the very edge of the fields, too close to the hedge to be harvested with a machine. This is called 'gleaning' and is still legal to this day, although it is far better to ask the farmer if you can go into the field after the harvester and 'glean' from the edges. You might just get enough to grind into flour for a loaf of bread.

A Story about Lughnasadh

This story takes place far away from this land, although some may say that the original Celtic people came from somewhere in the north of India many thousands of years ago. But let's come back to this age.

In a village in the Samba area of Kashmir is a village called Rehian. It's in a very green area of India, a very beautiful area. Lord Krishna High School is the main secondary school that young people go to in this area and it was at this school that Masmal met Neel. Both boys were the same age but very different because, unlike a lot of people that come from India, Neel had blue eyes! His skin was paler than Masmal's although his parents were both darker. It was just one of those happenings in nature that children can be born looking far more like one of their great grand-parents than their own parents.

The two became firm friends. They were in the same class, so they studied together and out of school they tried to meet up, but that was not always possible because Masmal came from a farming family and that meant he had a lot of chores to do once he left school. So at times Neel would go along and also help out. He enjoyed working on the farm.

They grew maize in some of the fields on Masmal's farm. It was a well known food in parts of India, but the reason Masmal's father grew it was a result of his time spent in America as a student. He had studied American farming methods and their different grains and when he came home, he made the choice of growing some on his own land.

Masmal was a strong boy. He was the eldest of his siblings and worked hard to help his father because he knew that one day the farm could be his and it would be his role to grow this grain. Not only was he strong, but unfortunately he had a temper as well, quite a fiery personality! And yet where Neel was concerned he was all feeling, he had taken to this friend very early on and there was something very beautiful about his eyes. They looked like the Sun shining onto the waters of the lake on a clear day. The two went everywhere together, to school, back home to help on the farm whenever possible.

One day Masmal came to school with a very sad look on his face. 'What's up with you?' asked Neel.

'My parents want my sister to get married and I think she is too young.'

'How old is she then?' asked Neel.

'She is fourteen and my parents say it's time for her to marry,' said Masmal.

Now we all know in Europe and in most parts of the world this would be far too young to marry, but in this culture it was normal for very young children to be 'married' although they did not set up home on their own. The girl would move into the family home of her new husband. To be honest, this could mean she was treated badly. Because she was the youngest woman in the home, she got the worst jobs and was at the beck and call of the older women.

'Is she like you?' Neel asked.

'Yes, in fact we look very much alike, so much so that as little children we were taken for twins,' said Masmal.

'I have the perfect answer then, I can marry her,' said Neel.

'You!' said Masmal.

'Why not?' Neel asked. 'If she is like you then I will get on with her very well and when we are older then we shall have beautiful children.'

Neel went home that day very happy with himself, he felt it was the least he could do for his best friend, and he was sure that his parents would be pleased to know that he would be settled and also pleased to have another person in the family to help in the home. Both Neel's parents were doctors and worked full time so to have someone at home to cook meals, clean the house and water the garden seemed like a wonderful idea.

But when he told his parents the story his parents were not at all happy with the idea! They never wanted Neel to marry early, they wanted him to go to university and study to be a doctor like them, perhaps marry another doctor or the daughter of the same kind of family. And so they put a stop to any ideas the boys had. But it never stopped at that. Neel's parents thought it was better that he did not spend so much time with Masmal and his family!

Well, as you can imagine there was a lot of heartache over all of this and in the end the two sets of parents got together and agreed that there would be no such marriage between the families, and that the boys would spend less time together. But they did agree to one thing, they could work together to harvest the maize as they had done the year before.

When the day came, the Sun was hot in the sky and the grains were ripe, strong plants and ready to be cut down. Masmal and Neel worked hard from early in the morning until late at night to bring in all the grain. The next day they went back into the field and cut the stalks and bound them with string into bales to be used for the animals in the months over winter.

After a week all the work was done and the day came for Neel to go back to his own home and leave Masmal and his family. If you think that boys don't cry, then you would be wrong! Both boys hugged each other and cried and then Neel left to go home to his own family and Masmal was left without his best friend, the person he felt so very close to.

After that terrible day Neel felt as if his friend had died. He felt grief for the first time. Although he knew his friend was at home with his family, Neel's heart felt as if it was broken.

Weeks went by and school started again. The boys had gone up into the next year and both felt older and different.

Masmal greeted his old friend warmly and they sat down together at the same table and at lunch time had the chance to talk. 'I went out with some of the grain we harvested after you left,' Masmal said to Neel. 'It's growing well and it looks as if we shall have a good crop next year. Will you help me gather in the harvest again next year?'

Neel suddenly felt a warmth building up inside him, where he had been so very sad the feeling was being replaced by a warm happiness. And at that point he knew he would always find the time to help his dearest friend with the harvest, even if it meant that each year when it was all over he would have to cope with the sadness at leaving him again.

'As long as I am able I will always help you gather in your harvest, because you are my very best friend and will be always,' Neel said.

The two boys hugged each other and this hug was the one that would seal a friendship for many years to come.

For each year the harvest needs to be cut down and gathered at Masmal's farm and each year wherever he is in the world, Neel takes some holiday and goes back to Rehian to stay with his friend and help him with the harvest.

Interesting Information You Can Find and Learn about Lughnasadh

1. Lughnasadh is also known as Lammas. It is the first of how many 'Harvest Festivals' that we can celebrate in the Pagan Wheel of the Year? What is harvested at this time of year?

2. As Pagans we understand that spirit is within all things. The Goddess knows that the spirit of her God, her partner, is in the plant which has to be cut down to be harvested. So we feel that part of the God gives his life to feed his people. Songs are sung about him and some give him a name. Can you write down one of the more famous names given to the God connected to this time of year? See if you can find the song that uses that name.

3. What kind of food is made from this type of harvest? Try making some of this food with the help of a grownup and then share your work with family or friends.

4. In the story about this time of year, the character Masmal's name spells something else, what is it?

5. Masmal lives in which country? And what crop does he help harvest? He has a friend who helps him and his name means 'blue' what is it?

(Write the answers in your notebook, if you can find pictures of the crops that are harvested at this time of the year, please stick them into your notebook.)

Autumn Equinox

We have now reached the last festival on the Wheel of the Year and have also travelled round to the Water element in the west in Europe. The Autumn Equinox falls around September 20th to 24th in the northern hemisphere. If you are in the southern hemisphere it happens between March 20th to 23rd. We have another time of perfect balance, of equal night and equal day.

Water is traditionally linked to the emotions, to empathy and sympathy. Many a teacher and healer has been born in a Water star sign; it gives them the ability to feel both their own emotions and feel the emotions of others around them. The season has reached the time when the leaves are starting to die off, there is a change in the air and the colours on the leaves have altered from green to shades of red, orange and yellow, soon to go to brown. Because different trees come into leaf at different times, they also start to change at different times and I clearly remember the lime trees coming into leaf very early and starting to change colour at this time of the year.

The traditional direction for Water is west. However it's just a matter of common sense and if your nearest stretch of water, such as a lake, river or the sea, is to the east of where you live, then you would place the element of Water there and move the Air element to the west. But for now let us presume that our nearest large area of water is to the west and this will tie in to the classic positions for the four elements.

This feeling of emotion, of empathy and sympathy will affect all the things we do at this time of year, our ceremonies and our day-to-day life.

A Story about the Autumn Equinox

Parts of North Rhine-Westphalia, in Germany, are forested and also have very beautiful lakes. One of these is Möhnesee, which lies next to a forest, the Arnsberger Wald. It's a very famous lake, it has a dam holding water for the surrounding area and during the Second World War it was bombed causing terrible flooding and loss of life. But these days it is all rebuilt and you can walk across the bridge of the dam towards the forest where there are benches to rest on.

My story is about a girl who lived in the village of Körbecke close by. She had a bike and loved to get away for a ride. She would stop by the side of the dam, eat her packed lunch and watch the wildlife. Her name was Atwer, but she was German and it sounds like 'Atver'.

Atwer was allowed a lot of freedom to get out and about. Her parents felt she was safe cycling to the edge of the dam and watching the birds on the water and listening to the sounds of nature.

One afternoon, just as the Sun was starting to get low in the sky, Atwer saw a movement from the forest, although she could not hear anything. She watched and the movement came closer and closer until she could see a large owl flying towards her. As the owl got closer it hooted and went to sit in a tree near to her. Atwer turned around slowly and for a moment both the owl and the girl looked straight into each other's eyes.

She knew that it would be getting towards dusk soon and she could not stay and watch any longer, so she turned around and spoke to the owl.

'Owl, I am sorry that I can't stay much longer and I do want us to be friends, so if I come back tomorrow a little earlier will you meet me here?' she asked.

The owl looked at her and moved her head, a quiet short 'hoot' was heard and Atwer took that to mean 'yes'.

So off she went home to her parents and to have an evening meal. She was not allowed out after dark without one of her parents so she found a book on owls from her mother's bookshelf and took it off to read all about owls.

The next day she took her bike and cycled back to the same spot and waited. She did not have to wait very long before a 'hoot' came from the direction of the forest and the owl swooped silently towards her and went to sit on the same branch as the day before. Then the owl started to make a strange sound and if you had heard it you would have said it was trying to talk.

'It's no good, I just don't understand what you are trying to tell me,' said Atwer. 'But I will listen carefully and see if I can feel what you are telling me.'

One of the reasons that Atwer liked being on her own was that she had been born with a gift, or some would say a curse, to feel what others were feeling. Her birthday was in late February and there are those who do say that this does make you a very emotional person, for this star sign is a Water sign and the element of Water gives us a great depth of empathy and feeling.

Atwer cleared her mind and concentrated on the feeling that was coming from the owl, and that felt like anxiety. The owl was worried about something and she needed some kind of help. Then within a moment the owl took off in the direction of the trees, still making the strange sound and adding a 'hoot'.

There was no way Atwer was going to follow the owl into the forest, not on her own, so she felt the best thing to do was to go home and talk to her parents about this and see if she could get her dad to come back to the dam with her and then perhaps both of them could follow the owl.

'I'll come back tomorrow Owl and bring my dad, then you can show us what it is you are worried about,' she said and the owl swooped back across the water, dipping low over the surface, then flew back past Atwer in a silent salute.

The evening meal that night was a very chatty one. It took Atwer quite a while to explain all of this to her parents and to try to impress on them that the owl really did need some kind of help. Her dad said it would do him good to have a cycle ride and it was Saturday tomorrow, so it was agreed that they would take a packed lunch and go back to Möhnesee and wait for the owl.

It turned out to be a chilly autumn day. Not many visitors were around at that time of the year, so Atwer and her father had a very good time cycling over to the dam. They were having their food when the 'hoot' came from the woods and a bird with a large wingspan flew silently towards them. It settled on the tree again and both Atwer and her dad put all their food back into the saddle bags and secured the bikes to the parking place. The whole time the owl waited patiently, but once they were finished, as if by some secret signal, the owl began to make the strange sounds again. The owl then flew onto a tree a short distance away and made the same little sounds.

'It's very anxious, it wants us to follow,' said Atwer to her dad.

'Then that is exactly what we are going to do,' said her dad. They then walked over to the tree where the owl was sitting and looked up.

'Lead the way dear owl and we will follow,' said Atwer. Before she finished the sentence the owl gave a hoot and flew into the forest, and both Atwer and her dad followed a little way behind.

As they walked there was a rustle in the grass and bushes under the tree and they stood quite still. It was a badger, snuffling around the earth looking for worms! It was a rare sight and they watched for a few moments before continuing their walk through the woods, all the while following the owl.

They had been walking along a path into the forest when the owl flew into the dense part of the trees and stopped. It made a screech and appeared to wait.

The two followed into the forest and found the owl sitting on a branch and across the tree lay a fallen branch, a very large one and as they looked up the trunk of the tree they saw a round opening in the upright trunk. The fallen branch was half blocking the hole and then they saw them, two little fluffy faces trying to peer out of the hole and unable to get out, nor was the adult owl able to get in.

'Look she's got little ones!' said Atwer in a loud whisper, 'and they are stuck inside the tree.'

'I can see, the fallen branch has come across the hole and it's far too big for me to move,' said her dad.

With that her dad walked back to the path, took out his mobile phone, pressed a few buttons and was quickly talking to the wildlife ranger for this part of the Arnsberger Wald. He told the ranger where they were and what the problem was. The ranger said he would meet them there in about twenty minutes and come to see for himself.

Atwer and her dad sat down on the ground at the edge of the wood and waited until the ranger appeared and then took him to the owl's tree home. The ranger and her dad talked together and came to the conclusion that if they tied some strong rope to the fallen branch, around another tree and tied it to the Land Rover that the ranger had driven, it would be possible to move the branch enough to give the owl access to her chicks.

It all took the rest of the afternoon and eventually the branch was moved and the owl could get back into the hole where her chicks were very pleased to see her.

Atwer and her dad got a lift back to where they had left their bikes as the light was starting to go. The Sun was hitting the sky at an angle which left a salmon pink tinge to the few clouds, it looked almost as if someone had set fire to the sky, but it was soon gone. They were just getting ready to begin the short cycle ride back to Körbecke when the owl swooped over their heads, made a dive into the grass and caught a little vole, she turned and flew back.

'That's the first good meal the chicks will have since the branch came down,' said Atwer's dad. And after that they cycled home to tell Atwer's mum all about their adventure.

Interesting Information You Can Find and Learn about the Autumn Equinox

1. This time of year is linked to the element of Water, how does this make us feel?

2. This is another Harvest Festival, but what do we harvest at this time of the year?

3. In many cultures rivers are sacred and are often thought to be Goddesses. One of the most famous Celtic Goddesses is Danu. She is also known as 'Danu of the Flowing Waters' because she is a river Goddess. Can you name at least one well known river named after her? Can you also write down where this river is? Where does it go?

4. If you live near a river try to find out if there is a Goddess linked to it and if so what her name is.

5. Danu is known in Pagan circles as a Mother Goddess especially linked to Ireland. There is a phrase for the people who follow her, in English its 'The Children of Danu', what is the Irish wording for this?

6. Some stories, or myths, say that each deity can shapeshift into a creature. Which creature does the story talk about? This gives us a great respect for animals, birds, fish and all of creation. Can you find a picture of a special animal associated with the Goddess Danu?

Questions and Answers

Here, for those using this book, including all the parents, teachers and guardians, are the questions from each section and the answers. The student will require a notebook with some plain pages in order to draw and illustrate some of the answers. There may be other accepted answers and this will depend on where you live, these are mine.

Answers to the Samhain Questions

1. All major religions have a time of the year to remember their ancestors, for Pagans it's October 31st. For established Christians it's on November 1st, which they call 'All Saints Day', followed by the 'All Souls Day' on November 2nd. Jewish people remember their dead, especially those who died in the Holocaust, less than a week after Passover, which is in the spring. There are other special days when people around the world remember their ancestors, can you find them? What are they called and when are they?

(Use a notebook to answer the questions)

Answers: Jewish Remembrance Day: On **Holocaust Martyrs' and Heroes' Remembrance Day***, less than a week after Passover, the people of Israel commune with the memory of the six million martyrs of the Jewish people who perished at the hands of the Nazis in the Holocaust. Modern rites of public bereavement and special ceremonies are held. On this day a siren is sounded at 10a.m., as the nation observes two minutes of silence, pledging 'to remember, and to remind others never to forget'.*

Autumnal Equinox Day (AAAA Shūbun no Hi?) around September 23rd. This national holiday was established in 1948 as a day on which to honour one's ancestors and remember the dead. Prior to 1948, the Autumn Equinox was an imperial ancestor worship festival called Shūki kōrei-sai.

2. How do other faiths remember their dead? Do they say prayers? Do they light candles? Write down in your notebook how other faiths celebrate their ancestors and loved ones who have died.

Answer:
Christian Catholic Prayer for the Dead
God our Father,
Your power brings us to birth,
Your providence guides our lives,
and by Your command we return to dust.

Lord, those who die still live in Your presence,
their lives change but do not end.
I pray in hope for my family,
relatives and friends,
and for all the dead known to You alone.

In company with Christ,
Who died and now lives,
may they rejoice in Your kingdom,
where all our tears are wiped away.
Unite us together again in one family,
to sing Your praise forever and ever.

Amen.

2. On the internet it is now possible to trace your own family back in most cases at least three generations. Can you do this? Draw a family tree and put in the names of your family going back at least three generations. This may help you feel more of a connection with your family who came before you. There is so much to find out about how they lived, worked and what their interests were. If you are adopted, then why not draw a family tree of your adopted parents?

Answer: Starting with yourself, put in the names of your mother and father, and then their parents:

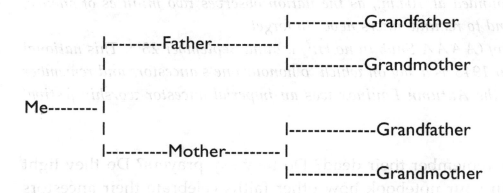

```
                                    |------------Grandfather
            |---------Father---------- |
            |                          |------------Grandmother
            |
Me--------- |
            |                          |-------------Grandfather
            |----------Mother--------- |
                                       |-------------Grandmother
```

3. Where did your ancestors live? In a house, a flat, a caravan or were they people who moved around and lived in different types of places?

Answer: In the UK, it's possible to find these answers by looking at past census records, which will give an address. The records for England and Wales up to 1911 can be found here: http://www.nationalarchives.gov.uk/records/census-records.htm. With this it's possible to find out how many people lived in the same building.

4. These days if someone dies we either bury them or cremate their body, while their spirit leaves and travels on to the Summerlands. Do you know where your ancestors, perhaps your great great grandparents, are buried or were cremated? Make a note of this in your notebook and, if you can, add a photo of the place.

Answer: You might find this information if you check burial records in the nearest church, cemetery or crematorium to where they lived. It's only in the last one hundred years that cremation has become accepted in Europe, even back fifty years it was not an acceptable method and yet in India and in other parts of the world this has been the accepted method of dealing with human remains. It was considered by some Celtic people that the soul of the departed would be released completely if their remains were cremated.

5. Some faiths and cultures give gifts of some kind to their ancestors. Find out about offerings made during the Mexican Day of the Dead festival or Chinese Spirit Money.

Answers: Offerings made during the Mexican Day of the Dead festival include flowers, especially marigolds. Toys are left for dead children. Sweets and drinks are also sometimes left. Another term for Chinese Spirit Money is Joss Paper. This is sheets of paper that are burnt for the dead at Chinese funerals.

Answers to the Yule Questions

1. We have a celebration, a family party four days after the Winter Solstice and we as Pagans call this 'Yule'. Other faiths also have a winter celebration and the best known one is 'Christ-Mass', now known as Christmas. Can you find out how many other faiths have a winter celebration? What do they call it? Write your answers in your notebook.

Answers: China: Signature of the Constitution of the Republic of China (Taiwan) on December 25th. This is a secular national holiday, which due to its date is celebrated in some respects like Christmas.

Hindu: 'Pancha Ganapati' a five-day festival in honour of Lord Ganesha who is Patron of Arts and Guardian of Culture on December 21st to 25th.

Hebrew:'Hanukkah', starting on 25th Kislev (Hebrew) or various dates in November or December is an eight-day festival commemorating the miracle of the oil after the desecration of the Temple in 165 BCE.

There are many other festivals to celebrate the Mid-winter in different countries all over the world and at different times, depending on when winter comes to that area. A look on Google will soon find several more.

2. At Midwinter we make a drink with spices and either red wine or redcurrant juice. We drink this warm, what is it called? The Germans have a special name for this hot winter drink, can you find out what this is called?

Answer: We call it simply mulled wine, but the Germans call it 'Glühwein' (gloo-vine) and it's a hot red wine that has been warmed with spices.

3. At this time of year we have less daylight. Can you keep a note of the time it becomes daylight and the time it gets dark for three days after the Midwinter Solstice? When the length of daylight gets longer, we can start the celebration of Yule. (Keep a note in your book of this in your book.)

Answer: This is something that can be done in a notebook, as it does require that the student writes the date and time of the sunrise and sunset for three to four days and then counts the amount of time in order to say for sure that daylight is increasing. Perhaps a simple cartoon strip would illustrate it?

4. Santa Claus is a story that comes from another country. Can you find out which country the story comes from? When do you think the well known Santa was painted with red and white clothes? Who started this red and white Santa?

Answer: The answer to this goes back to Europe to a story that you can find at http://www.whychristmas.com/customs/fatherchristmas.shtml

The Man behind the Story of Father Christmas or Santa Claus

St. Nicholas was a bishop who lived in the fourth century CE in a place called Myra in Asia Minor, now called Turkey. He was a very rich man because his parents died when he was young and left him a lot of money. He was also a very kind man and had a reputation for helping the poor by giving secret gifts to people who needed it. There are several legends about St. Nicholas, although because all this happened such a long time ago we don't have proof for all of this. It's a story that has been passed down by mouth from one generation to another through time.

This is from the Coca-Cola website: http://www.thecoca-colacompany.com/heritage/cokelore_santa.html

Coca-Cola® and Santa Claus

Most people can agree on what Santa Claus looks like - jolly, with a red suit and a white beard. But he did not always look that way, and Coca-Cola® advertising actually helped shape this modern-day image of Santa.

2006 marked the 75th anniversary of the famous Coca-Cola Santa Claus. Starting in 1931, magazine ads for Coca-Cola featured St. Nick as a kind, jolly man in a red suit. Because magazines were so widely viewed, and because this image of Santa appeared for more than three decades, the image of Santa most people have today is largely based on our advertising.

Before the 1931 introduction of the Coca-Cola Santa Claus created by artist Haddon Sundblom, the image of Santa ranged from big to small and fat to tall. Santa even appeared as an elf and looked a bit spooky.

Through the centuries, Santa Claus has been depicted as everything from a tall gaunt man to an elf. He has worn a bishop's robe and a Norse huntsman's animal skin. The modern-day Santa Claus is a combination of a number of the stories from a variety of countries. The Civil War cartoonist Thomas Nast drew Santa Claus for Harper's Weekly in 1862; Santa was shown as a small elf-like figure who supported the Union. Nast continued to draw Santa for 30 years and along the way changed the colour of his coat from tan to the now traditional red. Though some people believe the Coca-Cola Santa wears red because that is the Coke® colour, the red suit comes from Nast's interpretation of St. Nick.

5. Long ago boxes were given by the Lord of the Manor to his servants and to the poor of his village. These had little presents in them. This happened the day after 'Christ-Mass', which Pagans call 'Yule'. What is the day after Christmas day called now in modern times?

Answer: This is an answer that most children should be able to work out for themselves. The day after Christmas Day, December 25th, is called 'Boxing Day' and the name comes from the old tradition of giving boxes with little gifts on that day.

Answers to the Imbolc Questions

1. Imbolc is the time of year when we can see the very first early signs of spring. What flowers can you see at this time of year in your area? Are there other plants that show early signs of spring in your area?

Answers: The best known flower and the one which we associate with the Goddess Bridget is the snowdrop. In the UK it's the first little flower that can be seen often growing through the snow any time from early January onwards. There are many other early spring flowers, but it's the snowdrop that tops the list for the Pagan. There is a list of other early spring flowers on Wikipedia: http://en.wikipedia.org/wiki/List_of_early_spring_flowers

2. Mother sheep are called 'ewes'. They have their lambs in the spring time. If you have any farms with sheep near you, try to find out when the lambing starts in your area. What other animals usually give birth in the spring? Can you find out what animal gives birth the earliest in your area?

Answers: This answer will be different depending on how far above sea level you live. In low areas, closer to the sea, it is likely the lambs will be born very early and in some places farmers bring different breeds in to lambing sheds to lamb early so their lambs are big enough to go to market to be sold on in the autumn. These will lamb soon after Yule. But the most likely time you would find lambs is any time after the Spring Equinox.

3. There is a special Goddess we associate with this time of the year. she is called 'Brigit' or 'Bridget', and she was said to love animals, healing sick ones and helping the ewes give birth to the lambs. Where did she come from? Can you find out more about her?

Answer: There is a large section on Wikipedia that gives details about the Celtic Goddess Bridget who came from Ireland: http://en.wikipedia.org/wiki/Brigid

4. Many Pagans think of our Goddess as being a Maiden, a Mother and a Wise Woman. Can you find out which aspect of the Goddess we celebrate at this time of year? Is it Maiden, Mother, or Wise Woman?

Answer: In early spring we associate the Goddess to her 'Maiden' aspect. The colour of ribbons, flowers and candles used at this time of the year would be white. The person chosen to undertake roles in our group is a young girl and if necessary we would ask an older maid to assist her in the role.

5. There is a drink, a liquid which is connected to this time of year, what is it? How many different types of this drink have you tried? If you have never tried this drink, or only one type and you are not allergic to it, perhaps your parents will help you get some different types of this drink to taste.

Answer: Milk. If the student has never tried goats' milk then now would be a very good time to try some as this would be very similar to ewes' milk, although ewes' milk does have much more fat and is normally used to make cheese.

If the student has never drunk milk before, apart from their own mother's milk when they were a baby, and are not allergic to it, now is a great time to let them try it.

Answers to Spring Equinox Questions

2. The length of day and night are equal at this time of the year. What time does it get light and what time does it get too dark to see for driving? (This is known as 'lighting up time' and is when our parents, teachers and guardians have to put on the lights on their cars on to drive.) Keep a note of these times for three days.

Answers: This is a question that teachers will need to guide students with. First students should use a notebook and simply write down the times of dawn and sunset.

If they are old enough, teachers should help them to draw a graph with a dot at the times and then over three days they can join the dots and watch as the lines move further apart showing that its clearly getting lighter and the days are getting longer.

3. Find out more about the astronomy of equinoxes by looking them up on the internet or in a library.

Answer: An equinox occurs twice a year (around March 20th and September 22nd), when the tilt of the Earth's axis is inclined neither away from nor towards the Sun, the centre of the Sun being in the same plane as the Earth's equator. The term equinox can also be used in a broader sense, meaning the date when such a passage happens. The name 'equinox' is derived from the Latin aequus (equal) and nox (night), because around the equinox, the night and day have approximately equal length.

4. The Anglo Saxon Goddess who was said to bring the spring is called 'Ostara', which country did she come from?

Answer: She came from Germany in ancient times. See this link, which gives the other spelling of her name: http://en.wikipedia.org/wiki/%C4%92ostre

5. The hare is very special to Pagans and is connected to this celebration. Where do hares have their babies and what are they called? Find out if there is anywhere near you where you can see hares in the wild. If you want to find out more about hares try looking them up on the internet or in a library.

Answer: Teachers should encourage students to look for the answer for this either in the library or on the internet. The short answer is that they have their babies in dips or hollows in the ground and the baby hare is called a 'leveret'.

6. The egg is also linked to this time of year, why do you think this is? (Find out and write the answer in your notebook.)

Answer: The Easter Egg has pagan roots, even the word Easter has come to us from the Norsemen's Eostur, Eastar, Ostara, and Ostar, and the pagan goddess Eostre, all of which involve the season of the growing Sun and new birth. The egg is a symbol of new life, of fertility, which is why we make brightly coloured eggs at this time of the year.

7. We celebrate the arrival of spring at this time of year and we give children chocolate eggs. Christians also give eggs in the spring time but not at Ostara. When do they give eggs to their children? Do you know of any other faith that gives sweets or chocolate to children at special festivals in the year? Make a note of which other faiths do this and when in your notebook.

Answer: Easter has become a very secular holiday these days and most parents buy chocolate eggs and other sweets for their children at Easter in Europe.

In Germany and in other parts of Europe, children are given chocolate and sweets on the feast of St. Nicholas, which is December 6th.

Answers to Beltane Questions

1. We celebrate the joining of the God with the Goddess at this time of year. What is the name often given to the pagan wedding ceremony which joins two people in love?

Answer: Handfasting.

2. The festival falls on the Wheel of the Year between the element of Air, which we think of as yellow, and the element of Fire, which we think of as red. Paint or draw a Beltane picture using these colours. What other colours do you see in the world around you at this time of year?

Answer: There is no right or wrong answer to this question, it's very much up to the reader to undertake a piece of art which to them speaks of this time of year.

3. Beltane is very much a festival of love. Which flower would you associate with love? Where does this flowers come from? A tree? A bush? A bulb? Find or take a photo of a flower you think is associated with love?

Answer: My suggestion would be the rose and it grows on a bush. A photo of a red rose would be a good addition to your collection of answers to the questions.

4. Wiccans celebrate the joining of the God and Goddess; Druids go one step on from there, what do they celebrate or think of at this time of year?

Answer: Wiccans make a big point of celebrating the marriage of the Goddess with the God, but a Druid would be more concerned about the outcome of this union, the creation, be that a child, a story, a song or any other piece of creation.

5. In Scotland, UK, there is a well known fire festival at Beltane in Edinburgh. Try to find out what happened in areas of Scotland and Wales with livestock at this time of the year. Did fire play a special part in what happened?

Answer: The Beltane fire festival is an annual participatory arts event in Edinburgh, at which bonfires are lit. In the past, farmers would light fires and drive their cattle between them at Beltane. You could expand this and find out what happens in your part of the world at Beltane? Do the farmers take their cattle that have overwintered in sheds out into the fields for the summer? Are there bonfires or picnics?

Answers to Midsummer questions

1. The element for this time of year is Fire, we think of the heat of the Sun. How long is the length of day at this time of year? Make a note of when it becomes light and when it becomes dark at this time of year? (If you live in a far north part of the world, then make a note of when you start to see a little dark during the twenty-four hours.)

Answer: Midsummer comes at different times of the year depending on where you are living. In the UK it's around June 21st but you may be on the other side of the world, which would mean your Midsummer would be December 21st. If you live in the north of Norway, how long is your day? Do you have any dark at all? Make a note of the effect that Midsummer makes in your part of the world.

2. Which colour is associated with this element? And what direction is associated with Fire where you live?

Answer: On a Pagan Wheel of the Year the element colour would be red and in the UK or in Europe we would say that the South would be where the strength of the heat of the midday and Midsummer Sun is. But this again depends on where you live and if you are in Australia then perhaps your North would be where the hot, red part of your wheel lies. The answer is to write about where you live now.

3. Druids are well known for gathering together to celebrate the Midsummer sunrise, but where is the most well-known place where they do this? What was this place probably used for by our ancestors? Write the answer in your notebook.

Answer: Stonehenge. It is most likely a monument for our ancestors and in fact the most important time of the year would be Midwinter, as the Sun is reborn and with it the hope of our ancestors' future lives.

4. Midsummer is also known by another name, what is it? There are two of these in the year, what would the other one be called? When would the other one be? Draw a circle in your notebook and mark when these two celebrations are.

Answer: Summer Solstice. The other solstice is the Winter Solstice. Draw a circle and mark the two different festivals and indicate the colours that would illustrate the elements for them.

5. In early myths it was said that an animal pulled the Sun across the sky, which animal was this? Can you draw or photograph one of these and put it into your notebook?

Answer: Horse.

6. There is a play written about Midsummer by a very famous playwright. Can you find out what it is called and something about the story in the play?

Answer: 'A Midsummer's Night Dream' by William Shakespeare. The play is about a group of people lost in a forest on Midsummer night, and fairies who play tricks on them.

Answers to Lughnasadh Questions

1. Lughnasadh is also known as Lammas. It is the first of how many 'Harvest Festivals' that we celebrate on the Pagan Wheel of the Year. What is harvested at this time of year?

Answer: It is the grain harvest, often called the 'corn harvest'.

2. As Pagans we understand that spirit is within all things. The Goddess knows that the spirit of her God, her partner, is in the plant which has to be cut down to be harvested. So we feel that part of the God gives his life to feed his people. Songs are sung about him and some give him a name. Can you write down one of the more famous names given to the God connected to this time of year? See if you can find the song that uses that name.

Answer: 'John Barleycorn'. Here are the words:

There were three men came out of the west, their fortunes for to try

And these three men made a solemn vow

John Barleycorn must die

They've ploughed, they've sown, they've harrowed him in

Threw clods upon his head

And these three men made a solemn vow

John Barleycorn was dead

They've let him lie for a very long time, 'til the rains from heaven did fall

And little Sir John sprung up his head and so amazed them all

They've let him stand 'til Midsummer's Day 'til he looked both pale and wan

And little Sir John's grown a long long beard and so become a man

They've hired men with their scythes so sharp to cut him off at the knee

They've rolled him and tied him by the waist serving him most barbarously

They've hired men with their sharp pitchforks who've pricked him to the heart

And the loader he has served him worse than that

For he's bound him to the cart

They've wheeled him around and around a field 'til they came unto a barn

And there they made a solemn oath on poor John Barleycorn

They've hired men with their crabtree sticks to cut him skin from bone

And the miller he has served him worse than that

For he's ground him between two stones

And little Sir John and the nut brown bowl and his brandy in the glass

And little Sir John and the nut brown bowl proved the strongest man at last

The huntsman he can't hunt the fox nor so loudly to blow his horn

And the tinker he can't mend kettle or pots without a little barleycorn

3. What kind of food is made from this type of harvest? Try making some of this food with the help of a grownup and then share your work with family or friends.

Answer: You must find a recipe from your area of the world, but here is mine, it's sweetcorn pancakes.

2 tablespoons of yellow maize flour

2 tablespoons of self-raising flour

Pinch of salt

1 or 2 eggs, depending on the size

A glass of milk and a small tin of sweetcorn

Method:

Put all the dry ingredients into a bowl and make a dip or a well in the middle, break the eggs into a little bowl and then beat them with a fork and add the beaten egg a little at a time with some of the milk until the mixture is thick. Add in the sweetcorn and at this stage the mixture should fall off the spoon on the count of three if you hold a large spoon full above the bowl. Any quicker and the mixture is too thin and you need to add more flour, any longer and it's too thick and you need to add a little more milk or water.

Drop a tablespoon of the mixture into a hot pan with a little olive oil and fry until bubbles have risen to the top and then turn the pancake over and cook on the other side. Cook all the mixture in this way.

Eat and enjoy with your family and friends.

4. In the story about this time of year, the character Masmal's name spells something else, what is it?
Answer: Lammas.

5. Masmal lives in which country? And what crop does he help harvest? He has a friend who helps him and his name means 'blue' what is it? (Put the answers in your notebook, if you can find pictures of the crops that are harvested at this time of the year, please stick them into your notebook.)
Answers: He lives in India. The crops are maize or corn and the name of his friend is 'Neel'.

Answers to Autumn Equinox Questions

1. This time of year is linked to the element of Water, how does this make us feel?
Answer: Emotional.

2. This is another time of harvest, but what do we harvest at this time of the year?
Answer: It is the apple harvest.

3. In many cultures rivers are sacred and are often thought to be Goddesses. One of the most famous Celtic Goddesses is Danu, she is also known as 'Danu of the Flowing Waters' because she is a river Goddess. Can you name at least one well known river named after her? Can you also write down where this river is? Where does it go?
Answer: Danube. Here is the Wikipedia answer about the river Danube:
Classified as an international waterway, it originates in the town of Donaueschingen in the Black Forest of Germany, at the confluence of the rivers Brigach and Breg The Danube then flows southeast for 2,872 km (1,785 mi), passing through four Central European capitals before emptying into the Black Sea via the Danube Delta in Romania and Ukraine.

4. If you live near a river try to find out if there is a Goddess linked to it and if so

what her name is.

Answer: This is something you need to do yourself, I can only tell you my own answer which is: I live in Glasgow and the river Clyde runs through the city, the name of the river Goddess for the Clyde is 'Clutha'. (also known as: Clyde, Cliota, Clywd.)

5. 'Danu' is known in Pagan circles as a Mother Goddess especially linked to Ireland. There is a phrase for the people who follow her. In English it is 'The Children of Danu', what is the Irish wording for this?

Answer: Tuatha Dé Dannann.

6. Some stories and myths say that each Deity can shapeshift into a creature. Which creature does the story talk about? This gives us a great respect for animals, birds, fish and all of creation knowing that they all have a spark of the Divine within them. Can you find a picture of a special animal associated with the Goddess Danu?

Answer: Danu is said to shapeshift as a red female fox, a vixen.

Moon Books invites you to begin or deepen your encounter with

Paganism, in all its rich, creative, flourishing forms.

9781780995618